Wellbeing Journal – 52 week planner

Time can slip away without us actively working towards the things that are important to us. When we don't allow ourselves time to look at how we live our lives, we don't give ourselves space to choose what we really want. Big changes often fall short. But small, consistent changes can have a huge impact on our wellbeing and in obtaining our goals. This journal is for you to give yourself time and permission to really look at your life, and move in the direction you want to go. It is full of positive, inspirational quotes, encouraging you to look at your mindset and embrace habits that will enhance your wellbeing.

You will be encouraged to consider:
• Your goals and priorities.
• Your self-care, including sleep, diet, exercise, and relaxation.
• Your mind and mental wellbeing, including how you experience stress and utilise strategies, such as movement, mindfulness and breathing.
• Your relationships and gratitude for those in your life.

Through consistent journaling, you will gain clarity on where you are thriving and what you want to change. It is useful to record your wins and challenges on a weekly basis for you to identify, over time, what's working and what's not working. This process allows you to identify your patterns and gain insight for you to celebrate your wins, make small changes, and for you to live the life you want to live.

In the journal, there is space for you to plan, organise and schedule your time, manage your to-do lists, track your habits and journal in any way you feel will serve you.

Let's make the next 52 weeks count. Let's focus our energy to enhance our wellbeing and achieve great things. What will you choose? I hope you find inspiration and motivation to support you in taking positive steps to enhance your wellbeing and to live a more fulfilling life. Enjoy the process of self-discovery!

Hannah
Sensory Wellbeing OT

2023 Calendar

	Mon	Tue	Wed	Thu	Fri	Sat	Sun	Wk
	26	27	28	29	30	31	1	52
	2	3	4	5	6	7	8	1
January	9	10	11	12	13	14	15	2
	16	17	18	19	20	21	22	3
	23	24	25	26	27	28	29	4
	30	31	1	2	3	4	5	5
	6	7	8	9	10	11	12	6
February	13	14	15	16	17	18	19	7
	20	21	22	23	24	25	26	8
	27	28	1	2	3	4	5	9
	6	7	8	9	10	11	12	10
March	13	14	15	16	17	18	19	11
	20	21	22	23	24	25	26	12
	27	28	29	30	31	1	2	13
	3	4	5	6	7	8	9	14
April	10	11	12	13	14	15	16	15
	17	18	19	20	21	22	23	16
	24	25	26	27	28	29	30	17
	1	2	3	4	5	6	7	18
	8	9	10	11	12	13	14	19
May	15	16	17	18	19	20	21	20
	22	23	24	25	26	27	28	21
	29	30	31	1	2	3	4	22
	5	6	7	8	9	10	11	23
June	12	13	14	15	16	17	18	24
	19	20	21	22	23	24	25	25
	26	27	28	29	30	1	2	26

	Mon	Tue	Wed	Thu	Fri	Sat	Sun	Wk
July	3	4	5	6	7	8	9	27
	10	11	12	13	14	15	16	28
	17	18	19	20	21	22	23	29
	24	25	26	27	28	29	30	30
August	31	1	2	3	4	5	6	31
	7	8	9	10	11	12	13	32
	14	15	16	17	18	19	20	33
	21	22	23	24	25	26	27	34
	28	29	30	31	1	2	3	35
September	4	5	6	7	8	9	10	36
	11	12	13	14	15	16	17	37
	18	19	20	21	22	23	24	38
	25	26	27	28	29	30	1	39
October	2	3	4	5	6	7	8	40
	9	10	11	12	13	14	15	41
	16	17	18	19	20	21	22	42
	23	24	25	26	27	28	29	43
	30	31	1	2	3	4	5	44
November	6	7	8	9	10	11	12	45
	13	14	15	16	17	18	19	46
	20	21	22	23	24	25	26	47
	27	28	29	30	1	2	3	48
December	4	5	6	7	8	9	10	49
	11	12	13	14	15	16	17	50
	18	19	20	21	22	23	24	51
	25	26	27	28	29	30	31	52
	1	2	3	4	5	6	7	1

Where your focus goes your energy flows. Without focus or goals, time creeps away! What do you want to accomplish in the next 12 months? Where do you want to be in a year's time? What kind of life do you want to be living?

Monthly Planner

M	T	W	T	F	S	S

Goals and priorities this month

My Notes

Date:

Week Commencing   /   /

Top priority this week:

My 3 daily habits to track

1. ....

2. ....

3. ....

Tracker

M	T	W	T	F	S	S
M	T	W	T	F	S	S
M	T	W	T	F	S	S

To do

☐ _____
☐ _____
☐ _____
☐ _____
☐ _____
☐ _____
☐ _____
☐ _____

Notes

MONDAY

TUESDAY

WEDNESDAY

THURSDAY

FRIDAY

SATURDAY

SUNDAY

How I rate this week out of 5

1   2   3   4   5

"Many people limit themselves to what they think they can do. You can go as far as your mind lets you. What you believe, remember, you can achieve."

Mary Kay Ash

Week Commencing   /   /

Top priority this week:

My 3 daily habits to track

1. ....

2. ....

3. ....

Tracker

M	T	W	T	F	S	S
M	T	W	T	F	S	S
M	T	W	T	F	S	S

MONDAY

TUESDAY

WEDNESDAY

THURSDAY

FRIDAY

SATURDAY

SUNDAY

To do

_____

_____

_____

_____

_____

_____

_____

_____

Notes

How I rate this week out of 5

1   2   3   4   5

"Setting goals is the first step into turning the invisible into the visible."

Antony Robbins

Week Commencing   /   /

Top priority this week:

My 3 daily habits to track

1. ....

2. ....

3. ....

Tracker

M	T	W	T	F	S	S
M	T	W	T	F	S	S
M	T	W	T	F	S	S

To do

_____

_____

_____

_____

_____

_____

_____

_____

Notes

MONDAY

TUESDAY

WEDNESDAY

THURSDAY

FRIDAY

SATURDAY

SUNDAY

How I rate this week out of 5

1   2   3   4   5

"A goal is a dream with a deadline."

Napoleon Hill

Week Commencing   /   /

Top priority this week:

My 3 daily habits to track

1. ....

2. ....

3. ....

Tracker

M	T	W	T	F	S	S
M	T	W	T	F	S	S
M	T	W	T	F	S	S

To do

_____

_____

_____

_____

_____

_____

_____

_____

Notes

MONDAY	
TUESDAY	
WEDNESDAY	
THURSDAY	
FRIDAY	
SATURDAY	
SUNDAY	

How I rate this week out of 5

1   2   3   4   5

"Success is easy to achieve once you set your mind on a specific goal."

Aristotle

What do you prioritise on a day-to-day basis? It's important to think about what your priorities are, so you make space for these in your life. All too often we are busy filling our lives with the things that are not important to us. How can you master the major things in life, not the minor things in life?

Monthly Planner

M	T	W	T	F	S	S

Goals and priorities this month

My Notes

Date:

_____

_____

_____

_____

_____

_____

_____

_____

_____

_____

_____

_____

_____

_____

_____

_____

_____

_____

_____

_____

_____

Week Commencing   /   /

Top priority this week:

My 3 daily habits to track

1. ....

2. ....

3. ....

Tracker

M	T	W	T	F	S	S
M	T	W	T	F	S	S
M	T	W	T	F	S	S

To do

_____
_____
_____
_____
_____
_____
_____
_____

Notes

MONDAY

TUESDAY

WEDNESDAY

THURSDAY

FRIDAY

SATURDAY

SUNDAY

How I rate this week out of 5

1   2   3   4   5

"You have to decide what your highest priorities are and have the courage – pleasantly, smilingly, non-apologetically – to say NO to other things. And the way to do that is by having a bigger YES burning inside."

Stephen Co ey

Week Commencing / /

Top priority this week:

My 3 daily habits to track

1. ....

2. ....

3. ....

Tracker

M	T	W	T	F	S	S
M	T	W	T	F	S	S
M	T	W	T	F	S	S

To do

_____
_____
_____
_____
_____
_____
_____
_____

MONDAY	
TUESDAY	
WEDNESDAY	
THURSDAY	
FRIDAY	
SATURDAY	
SUNDAY	

Notes

How I rate this week out of 5

1   2   3   4   5

"Action expresses priorities."

Mahatma Gandhi.

Week Commencing / /

Top priority this week:

My 3 daily habits to track

1. ....

2. ....

3. ....

Tracker

M	T	W	T	F	S	S
M	T	W	T	F	S	S
M	T	W	T	F	S	S

To do

_____

_____

_____

_____

_____

_____

_____

_____

Notes

MONDAY

TUESDAY

WEDNESDAY

THURSDAY

FRIDAY

SATURDAY

SUNDAY

How I rate this week out of 5

1   2   3   4   5

"When you know what is important to you, making a decision is quite simple."

Tony Robbins

Week Commencing   /   /

Top priority this week:

My 3 daily habits to track

1. ....

2. ....

3. ....

Tracker

M   T   W   T   F   S   S

M   T   W   T   F   S   S

M   T   W   T   F   S   S

To do

_____

_____

_____

_____

_____

_____

_____

_____

Notes

MONDAY

TUESDAY

WEDNESDAY

THURSDAY

FRIDAY

SATURDAY

SUNDAY

How I rate this week out of 5

1   2   3   4   5

"To change your life, you need to change your priorities."

Mark Twain

Declutter your mind and your space. What needs to go? What can you let go of? What isn't serving you? Decluttering can be a springboard for change and new beginnings. What is weighing you down that you can change?

Monthly Planner

M	T	W	T	F	S	S

Goals and priorities this month

My Notes

Date:

_____

_____

_____

_____

_____

_____

_____

_____

_____

_____

_____

_____

_____

_____

_____

_____

_____

_____

_____

Week Commencing   /   /

Top priority this week:

My 3 daily habits to track

1. ....

2. ....

3. ....

Tracker

M	T	W	T	F	S	S

M	T	W	T	F	S	S

M	T	W	T	F	S	S

MONDAY

TUESDAY

WEDNESDAY

THURSDAY

FRIDAY

SATURDAY

SUNDAY

To do

_____

_____

_____

_____

_____

_____

_____

_____

Notes

How I rate this week out of 5

1   2   3   4   5

"The question of what you want to own is also the question of how you want to live your life."
Marie Kondo

Week Commencing   / /

Top priority this week:

My 3 daily habits to track

1. ....

2. ....

3. ....

Tracker

M	T	W	T	F	S	S
M	T	W	T	F	S	S
M	T	W	T	F	S	S

To do

_____

_____

_____

_____

_____

_____

_____

_____

Notes

MONDAY	
TUESDAY	
WEDNESDAY	
THURSDAY	
FRIDAY	
SATURDAY	
SUNDAY	

How I rate this week out of 5

1   2   3   4   5

"Under the influence of clutter, we may underestimate how much time we are giving to the less important stuff."

Zoë Kim

Week Commencing / /

Top priority this week:

My 3 daily habits to track

1. ....

2. ....

3. ....

Tracker

M	T	W	T	F	S	S

M	T	W	T	F	S	S

M	T	W	T	F	S	S

MONDAY

TUESDAY

WEDNESDAY

THURSDAY

FRIDAY

SATURDAY

SUNDAY

To do

_____

_____

_____

_____

_____

_____

_____

_____

Notes

How I rate this week out of 5

1   2   3   4   5

"Edit your life frequently and ruthlessly. It's your masterpiece after all."

Nathan W. Morris

Week Commencing / /

Top priority this week:

My 3 daily habits to track

1. ....

2. ....

3. ....

Tracker

M	T	W	T	F	S	S
M	T	W	T	F	S	S
M	T	W	T	F	S	S

To do

_____

_____

_____

_____

_____

_____

_____

_____

Notes

MONDAY

TUESDAY

WEDNESDAY

THURSDAY

FRIDAY

SATURDAY

SUNDAY

How I rate this week out of 5

1   2   3   4   5

"I am not what happened to me, I am what I choose to become."

Carl Jung

Week Commencing / /

Top priority this week:

My 3 daily habits to track

1. ....

2. ....

3. ....

Tracker

M	T	W	T	F	S	S

M	T	W	T	F	S	S

M	T	W	T	F	S	S

MONDAY

TUESDAY

WEDNESDAY

THURSDAY

FRIDAY

SATURDAY

SUNDAY

To do

_____

_____

_____

_____

_____

_____

_____

_____

Notes

How I rate this week out of 5

1   2   3   4   5

"I am not what happened to me, I am what I choose to become."

Carl Jung

Sunlight and sleep - are you getting enough? Getting morning sunlight in the eyes sets our circadian rhythm, influencing our sleep-wake cycle. Early morning sunlight from being outside triggers when our melatonin is released in the evening to help prepare the body for sleep. Sleep is vital to our wellbeing and longevity.

How is your sleep?

What can you do to improve it?

Monthly Planner

M	T	W	T	F	S	S

Goals and priorities this month

My Notes

Date:

Week Commencing   /   /

Top priority this week:

My 3 daily habits to track

1. ....

2. ....

3. ....

Tracker

M	T	W	T	F	S	S

M	T	W	T	F	S	S

M	T	W	T	F	S	S

To do

_____

_____

_____

_____

_____

_____

_____

_____

Notes

MONDAY

TUESDAY

WEDNESDAY

THURSDAY

FRIDAY

SATURDAY

SUNDAY

How I rate this week out of 5

1   2   3   4   5

"Sleep is an investment in the energy you need to be effective tomorrow."

Tom Roth

Week Commencing / /

Top priority this week:

My 3 daily habits to track

1. ....

2. ....

3. ....

Tracker

M	T	W	T	F	S	S
M	T	W	T	F	S	S
M	T	W	T	F	S	S

To do

_____

_____

_____

_____

_____

_____

_____

_____

Notes

MONDAY

TUESDAY

WEDNESDAY

THURSDAY

FRIDAY

SATURDAY

SUNDAY

How I rate this week out of 5

1   2   3   4   5

"Sleep has been provided by nature to do the body's healing work, and it takes seven or eight hours for this process to happen. Commit to getting at least seven to eight hours of good quality sleep every night to keep your body and hormones in balance."

Suzanne Somers

Week Commencing   /   /

Top priority this week:

My 3 daily habits to track

1. ....

2. ....

3. ....

Tracker

M	T	W	T	F	S	S

M	T	W	T	F	S	S

M	T	W	T	F	S	S

To do

_____
_____
_____
_____
_____
_____
_____
_____

Notes

MONDAY

TUESDAY

WEDNESDAY

THURSDAY

FRIDAY

SATURDAY

SUNDAY

How I rate this week out of 5

1   2   3   4   5

"By helping us keep the world in perspective, sleep gives us a chance to refocus on the essence of who we are. And in that place of connection, it is easier for the fears and concerns of the world to drop away."

Ariana Huffington

Week Commencing   /   /

Top priority this week:

My 3 daily habits to track

1. ....

2. ....

3. ....

Tracker

M	T	W	T	F	S	S
M	T	W	T	F	S	S
M	T	W	T	F	S	S

To do

- _____
- _____
- _____
- _____
- _____
- _____
- _____
- _____

Notes

MONDAY	
TUESDAY	
WEDNESDAY	
THURSDAY	
FRIDAY	
SATURDAY	
SUNDAY	

How I rate this week out of 5

1   2   3   4   5

"High-quality sleep fortifies your immune system, balances your hormones, boosts your metabolism, increases physical energy, and improves the function of your brain."

Shawn Ste enson

A healthy, balanced diet, rich in nutrient-dense foods gives the body what it needs to function and thrive. Think about what you feed your body. Is it health-giving or health-taking? Do you feel energised from your food throughout the day? What can you do to improve your nutrition? What does your body need?

Monthly Planner

M	T	W	T	F	S	S

Goals and priorities this month

My Notes

Date:

_____

_____

_____

_____

_____

_____

_____

_____

_____

_____

_____

_____

_____

_____

_____

_____

_____

_____

_____

_____

_____

_____

Week Commencing / /

Top priority this week:

My 3 daily habits to track

1. ....
2. ....
3. ....

Tracker

M	T	W	T	F	S	S
M	T	W	T	F	S	S
M	T	W	T	F	S	S

MONDAY	
TUESDAY	
WEDNESDAY	
THURSDAY	
FRIDAY	
SATURDAY	
SUNDAY	

To do

_____
_____
_____
_____
_____
_____
_____
_____

Notes

How I rate this week out of 5

1   2   3   4   5

"Healthy eating is a way of life, so it's important to establish routines that are simple, realistically, and ultimately liveable."

Horace

Week Commencing / /

Top priority this week:

My 3 daily habits to track

1. ....
2. ....
3. ....

Tracker

M	T	W	T	F	S	S
M	T	W	T	F	S	S
M	T	W	T	F	S	S

To do

_____

_____

_____

_____

_____

_____

_____

_____

Notes

MONDAY

TUESDAY

WEDNESDAY

THURSDAY

FRIDAY

SATURDAY

SUNDAY

How I rate this week out of 5

1   2   3   4   5

"Treat yourself as if you already are enough. Walk as if you are enough. Eat as if you are enough. See, look, listen as if you are enough. Because it's true."

Geneen Roth

Week Commencing / /

Top priority this week:

My 3 daily habits to track

1. ....

2. ....

3. ....

Tracker

M	T	W	T	F	S	S
M	T	W	T	F	S	S
M	T	W	T	F	S	S

MONDAY	
TUESDAY	
WEDNESDAY	
THURSDAY	
FRIDAY	
SATURDAY	
SUNDAY	

To do

_____

_____

_____

_____

_____

_____

_____

_____

Notes

How I rate this week out of 5

1   2   3   4   5

"We're all familiar with the idea that lifestyle can be the cause of disease. What's not common knowledge is that a change in lifestyle can also be the treatment and prevent us from getting sick in the first place."

Rangan Chatterjee

Week Commencing   / /

Top priority this week:

My 3 daily habits to track

1. ....

2. ....

3. ....

Tracker

M	T	W	T	F	S	S
M	T	W	T	F	S	S
M	T	W	T	F	S	S

To do

_____

_____

_____

_____

_____

_____

_____

_____

MONDAY

TUESDAY

WEDNESDAY

THURSDAY

FRIDAY

SATURDAY

SUNDAY

Notes

How I rate this week out of 5

1   2   3   4   5

"Let food be thy medicine, thy medicine shall be thy food."

Hippocrates

Our bodies need movement to maintain a level of fitness, good health and to achieve mental wellbeing. Whether it's 10k steps a day or chair yoga, are you allowing your body to exercise? Do you listen to your body or do you ignore it? What is your body trying to tell you?

Monthly Planner

M	T	W	T	F	S	S

Goals and priorities this month

My Notes

Date:

_____

_____

_____

_____

_____

_____

_____

_____

_____

_____

_____

_____

_____

_____

_____

_____

_____

_____

_____

_____

Week Commencing   / /

Top priority this week:

My 3 daily habits to track

1. ....

2. ....

3. ....

Tracker

M	T	W	T	F	S	S

M	T	W	T	F	S	S

M	T	W	T	F	S	S

MONDAY

TUESDAY

WEDNESDAY

THURSDAY

FRIDAY

SATURDAY

SUNDAY

To do

_____

_____

_____

_____

_____

_____

_____

_____

Notes

How I rate this week out of 5

1   2   3   4   5

"We are what we repeatedly do. Excellence, then, is not an act but a habit."

Aristotle

Week Commencing   /   /

Top priority this week:

My 3 daily habits to track

1. ....

2. ....

3. ....

Tracker

M	T	W	T	F	S	S

M	T	W	T	F	S	S

M	T	W	T	F	S	S

To do

_____

_____

_____

_____

_____

_____

_____

_____

Notes

MONDAY

TUESDAY

WEDNESDAY

THURSDAY

FRIDAY

SATURDAY

SUNDAY

How I rate this week out of 5

1   2   3   4   5

"The only person you are destined to become is the person you decide to be."

Ralph Waldo Emerson

Week Commencing   /   /

Top priority this week:

My 3 daily habits to track

1. ....
2. ....
3. ....

Tracker

M	T	W	T	F	S	S

M	T	W	T	F	S	S

M	T	W	T	F	S	S

MONDAY

TUESDAY

WEDNESDAY

THURSDAY

FRIDAY

SATURDAY

SUNDAY

To do

_____
_____
_____
_____
_____
_____
_____
_____

Notes

How I rate this week out of 5

1   2   3   4   5

¨The only person you are destined to become is the person you decide to be."

Ralph Waldo Emerson

Week Commencing   /   /

Top priority this week:

My 3 daily habits to track

1. ....

2. ....

3. ....

Tracker

M	T	W	T	F	S	S
M	T	W	T	F	S	S
M	T	W	T	F	S	S

MONDAY

TUESDAY

WEDNESDAY

THURSDAY

FRIDAY

SATURDAY

SUNDAY

To do

_____
_____
_____
_____
_____
_____
_____
_____

Notes

How I rate this week out of 5

1   2   3   4   5

"Take care of your body. It's the only place you have to live."

Jim Rohn

Week Commencing   /   /

Top priority this week:

My 3 daily habits to track

1. ....

2. ....

3. ....

Tracker

M	T	W	T	F	S	S
M	T	W	T	F	S	S
M	T	W	T	F	S	S

To do

_____
_____
_____
_____
_____
_____
_____
_____

Notes

MONDAY	
TUESDAY	
WEDNESDAY	
THURSDAY	
FRIDAY	
SATURDAY	
SUNDAY	

How I rate this week out of 5

1   **2**   **3**   **4**   **5**

"Our bodies are our gardens to which our wills are gardeners."

William Shakespeare

Take time to look within. How are you? How is your mind? Do you feel you are always racing but never where you want to be, despite all your efforts? Give yourself time for stillness. Give yourself permission to have space just to be — no judgement and no guilt. Notice where your mind shifts. Use mindfulness to be present in the now, without focusing on the past or future. Can you embrace your now?

Monthly Planner

M	T	W	T	F	S	S

Goals and priorities this month

My Notes

Date:

_____

_____

_____

_____

_____

_____

_____

_____

_____

_____

_____

_____

_____

_____

_____

_____

_____

_____

_____

_____

Week Commencing   /   /

Top priority this week:

My 3 daily habits to track

1. ....

2. ....

3. ....

Tracker

M	T	W	T	F	S	S

M	T	W	T	F	S	S

M	T	W	T	F	S	S

MONDAY

TUESDAY

WEDNESDAY

THURSDAY

FRIDAY

SATURDAY

SUNDAY

To do

_____

_____

_____

_____

_____

_____

_____

_____

Notes

How I rate this week out of 5

1   2   3   4   5

"There is no reality except the one contained within us."

Hermann Hesse

Week Commencing   /   /

Top priority this week:

My 3 daily habits to track

1. ....

2. ....

3. ....

Tracker

M	T	W	T	F	S	S
M	T	W	T	F	S	S
M	T	W	T	F	S	S

To do

_____
_____
_____
_____
_____
_____
_____
_____

Notes

MONDAY	
TUESDAY	
WEDNESDAY	
THURSDAY	
FRIDAY	
SATURDAY	
SUNDAY	

How I rate this week out of 5

1   2   3   4   5

"Watch your thoughts, for they become words. Watch your words, for they become actions. Watch your actions, for they become character. Watch your character, for it becomes your destiny."

Frank Outlaw

Week Commencing   /   /

Top priority this week:

My 3 daily habits to track

1. ....

2. ....

3. ....

Tracker

M	T	W	T	F	S	S

M	T	W	T	F	S	S

M	T	W	T	F	S	S

MONDAY

TUESDAY

WEDNESDAY

THURSDAY

FRIDAY

SATURDAY

SUNDAY

To do

_____

_____

_____

_____

_____

_____

_____

_____

Notes

How I rate this week out of 5

1   2   3   4   5

"The body benefits from movement, and the mind benefits from stillness."

Sakyong Miphan

Week Commencing   /   /

Top priority this week:

My 3 daily habits to track

1. ....

2. ....

3. ....

Tracker

M	T	W	T	F	S	S
M	T	W	T	F	S	S
M	T	W	T	F	S	S

To do

_____

_____

_____

_____

_____

_____

_____

_____

Notes

MONDAY	
TUESDAY	
WEDNESDAY	
THURSDAY	
FRIDAY	
SATURDAY	
SUNDAY	

How I rate this week out of 5

1   2   3   4   5

"To the mind that is still the whole universe surrenders."

Lao Tzu

Find your people — those that understand you and your experience in life. We are all different. Who makes you feel seen and accepted? Think of people in your life you are grateful for. How do they enrich your life? How do you show them your gratitude? Do you need to find other people in your life to feel seen and understood or have you found your people?

Monthly Planner

M	T	W	T	F	S	S

Goals and priorities this month

My Notes

Date:

_____

_____

_____

_____

_____

_____

_____

_____

_____

_____

_____

_____

_____

_____

_____

_____

_____

_____

_____

Week Commencing   /   /

Top priority this week:

My 3 daily habits to track

1. ....

2. ....

3. ....

Tracker

M	T	W	T	F	S	S

M	T	W	T	F	S	S

M	T	W	T	F	S	S

MONDAY

TUESDAY

WEDNESDAY

THURSDAY

FRIDAY

SATURDAY

SUNDAY

To do

_____

_____

_____

_____

_____

_____

_____

_____

Notes

How I rate this week out of 5

1   2   3   4   5

"Look for people in your life ... who will help calm the storms in your soul rather than challenge it to a battle."

Timothy Pina

Week Commencing   /   /

Top priority this week:

My 3 daily habits to track

1. ....

2. ....

3. ....

Tracker

M	T	W	T	F	S	S

M	T	W	T	F	S	S

M	T	W	T	F	S	S

MONDAY

TUESDAY

WEDNESDAY

THURSDAY

FRIDAY

SATURDAY

SUNDAY

To do

_____

_____

_____

_____

_____

_____

_____

Notes

How I rate this week out of 5

1   2   3   4   5

"End the day with gratitude. There is someone, somewhere that has less than you."

Zig Ziglar

Week Commencing   / /

Top priority this week:

My 3 daily habits to track

1. ....

2. ....

3. ....

Tracker

M	T	W	T	F	S	S
M	T	W	T	F	S	S
M	T	W	T	F	S	S

MONDAY

TUESDAY

WEDNESDAY

THURSDAY

FRIDAY

SATURDAY

SUNDAY

To do

_____

_____

_____

_____

_____

_____

_____

_____

Notes

How I rate this week out of 5

1   2   3   4   5

"There is a calmness to a life lived in gratitude, a quiet joy."

Ralph Blum

Week Commencing / /

Top priority this week:

My 3 daily habits to track

1. ....

2. ....

3. ....

Tracker

M	T	W	T	F	S	S
M	T	W	T	F	S	S
M	T	W	T	F	S	S

To do

- _____
- _____
- _____
- _____
- _____
- _____
- _____

Notes

MONDAY

TUESDAY

WEDNESDAY

THURSDAY

FRIDAY

SATURDAY

SUNDAY

How I rate this week out of 5

1   2   3   4   5

"The energy of gratitude catapults us into the most profound experiences imaginable."

James Tyman

Relax.

It's important that we allow ourselves to relax, to switch off from the demands of everyday life. How do you relax?

Is your chosen form of relaxation having a positive effect on your health and wellbeing or depleting it?

Could using technology for relaxation be perceived by your brain as stress? Can you find alternative ways to relax? Perhaps take a stroll where there is nature, get cosy on the sofa with a book or play an instrument.

Relaxation is an important component of our wellbeing. How can you incorporate relaxation into your routine?

Monthly Planner

M	T	W	T	F	S	S

Goals and priorities this month

My Notes

Date:

Week Commencing   /   /

Top priority this week:

My 3 daily habits to track

1. ....

2. ....

3. ....

Tracker

M	T	W	T	F	S	S
M	T	W	T	F	S	S
M	T	W	T	F	S	S

To do

_____
_____
_____
_____
_____
_____
_____
_____

Notes

MONDAY

TUESDAY

WEDNESDAY

THURSDAY

FRIDAY

SATURDAY

SUNDAY

How I rate this week out of 5

1   2   3   4   5

"Life isn't as serious as the mind makes it out to be."

Eckhart Tolle

Week Commencing   /   /

Top priority this week:

My 3 daily habits to track

1. ....

2. ....

3. ....

Tracker

M T W T F S S

M T W T F S S

M T W T F S S

MONDAY	
TUESDAY	
WEDNESDAY	
THURSDAY	
FRIDAY	
SATURDAY	
SUNDAY	

To do

_____

_____

_____

_____

_____

_____

_____

_____

Notes

How I rate this week out of 5

1   2   3   4   5

"The time to relax is when you don't have time for it."

Sydney Harris

Week Commencing   /   /

Top priority this week:

My 3 daily habits to track

1. ....

2. ....

3. ....

Tracker

M	T	W	T	F	S	S

M	T	W	T	F	S	S

M	T	W	T	F	S	S

MONDAY

TUESDAY

WEDNESDAY

THURSDAY

FRIDAY

SATURDAY

SUNDAY

To do

- _____
- _____
- _____
- _____
- _____
- _____
- _____
- _____

Notes

How I rate this week out of 5

1   2   3   4   5

"We will be more successful in all our endeavours if we can let go of the habit of running all the time, and take little pauses to relax and re-center ourselves. And we'll also have a lot more joy in living."

Thich Nhat Hanh

Week Commencing   /   /

Top priority this week:

My 3 daily habits to track

1. ....

2. ....

3. ....

Tracker

M	T	W	T	F	S	S
M	T	W	T	F	S	S
M	T	W	T	F	S	S

To do

_____

_____

_____

_____

_____

_____

_____

Notes

MONDAY	
TUESDAY	
WEDNESDAY	
THURSDAY	
FRIDAY	
SATURDAY	
SUNDAY	

How I rate this week out of 5

1   2   3   4   5

"Sometimes the most productive thing to do is relax."

Mark Black

Our breath is autonomic — we use it without conscious effort. Our breath has so much power in keeping us alive yet we often overlook it. We can harness the power of our breath to change our state of mind and induce positive effects on our body. Take time to notice your breath, focus on breathing deeply. With each inhalation, visualise positive energy entering your body, and with each exhalation, release any negative energy or emotions that aren't serving you.

Monthly Planner

M	T	W	T	F	S	S

Goals and priorities this month

My Notes

Date:

_____

_____

_____

_____

_____

_____

_____

_____

_____

_____

_____

_____

_____

_____

_____

_____

_____

_____

_____

_____

_____

Week Commencing   / /

Top priority this week:

My 3 daily habits to track

1. ....

2. ....

3. ....

Tracker

M	T	W	T	F	S	S
M	T	W	T	F	S	S
M	T	W	T	F	S	S

MONDAY

TUESDAY

WEDNESDAY

THURSDAY

FRIDAY

SATURDAY

SUNDAY

To do

_____

_____

_____

_____

_____

_____

_____

_____

Notes

How I rate this week out of 5

1   2   3   4   5

"Conscious breathing heightens awareness and deepens relaxation."

Dan Brule

Week Commencing   /   /

Top priority this week:

My 3 daily habits to track

1. ....
2. ....
3. ....

Tracker

M T W T F S S

M T W T F S S

M T W T F S S

| MONDAY |
| TUESDAY |
| WEDNESDAY |
| THURSDAY |
| FRIDAY |
| SATURDAY |
| SUNDAY |

To do

_____
_____
_____
_____
_____
_____
_____
_____

Notes

How I rate this week out of 5

1   2   3   4   5

"Breathing in, I calm body and mind. Breathing out, I smile. Dwelling in the present moment, I know this is the only moment."

Thich Nhat Hanh

Week Commencing / /

Top priority this week:

My 3 daily habits to track

1. ....

2. ....

3. ....

Tracker

M	T	W	T	F	S	S

M	T	W	T	F	S	S

M	T	W	T	F	S	S

MONDAY

TUESDAY

WEDNESDAY

THURSDAY

FRIDAY

SATURDAY

SUNDAY

To do

_____

_____

_____

_____

_____

_____

_____

_____

Notes

How I rate this week out of 5

1   2   3   4   5

"Breathing in, I calm body and mind. Breathing out, I smile. Dwelling in the present moment, I know this is the only moment."

Thich Nhat Hanh

Week Commencing   /   /

Top priority this week:

My 3 daily habits to track

1. ....

2. ....

3. ....

Tracker

M T W T F S S

M T W T F S S

M T W T F S S

MONDAY	
TUESDAY	
WEDNESDAY	
THURSDAY	
FRIDAY	
SATURDAY	
SUNDAY	

To do

_____

_____

_____

_____

_____

_____

_____

_____

Notes

How I rate this week out of 5

1   2   3   4   5

"If you want to conquer the anxiety of life, live in the moment, live in the breath."

Amit Ray

Week Commencing / /

Top priority this week:

My 3 daily habits to track

1. ....

2. ....

3. ....

Tracker

M	T	W	T	F	S	S
M	T	W	T	F	S	S
M	T	W	T	F	S	S

MONDAY

TUESDAY

WEDNESDAY

THURSDAY

FRIDAY

SATURDAY

SUNDAY

To do

_____

_____

_____

_____

_____

_____

_____

Notes

How I rate this week out of 5

1   2   3   4   5

"Our breathing has the ability to enlighten and activate any physiological mechanism in conscious control."

Wim Hoff

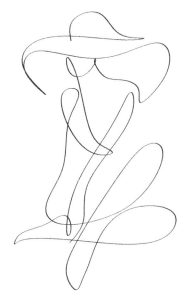

Stress is the health epidemic of modern-day society. Whether it's a genuine stressful event or just a notification on our smart phone, we are inundated with perceived stress throughout the day. How much stress do you experience on a typical day? What action can you take to reduce your stress exposure and simultaneously improve your wellbeing?

Monthly Planner

M	T	W	T	F	S	S

Goals and priorities this month

My Notes

Date:

_____

_____

_____

_____

_____

_____

_____

_____

_____

_____

_____

_____

_____

_____

_____

_____

_____

_____

_____

_____

Week Commencing   /   /

Top priority this week:

My 3 daily habits to track

1. ....

2. ....

3. ....

Tracker

M	T	W	T	F	S	S
M	T	W	T	F	S	S
M	T	W	T	F	S	S

To do

_____

_____

_____

_____

_____

_____

_____

MONDAY

TUESDAY

WEDNESDAY

THURSDAY

FRIDAY

SATURDAY

SUNDAY

Notes

How I rate this week out of 5

1   2   3   4   5

"Remember that stress doesn't come from what's going on in your life. It comes from your thoughts about what's going on in your life."

Andrew J. Bernstein

Week Commencing   / /

Top priority this week:

My 3 daily habits to track

1. ....
2. ....
3. ....

Tracker

M	T	W	T	F	S	S
M	T	W	T	F	S	S
M	T	W	T	F	S	S

MONDAY

TUESDAY

WEDNESDAY

THURSDAY

FRIDAY

SATURDAY

SUNDAY

To do

_____
_____
_____
_____
_____
_____
_____
_____

Notes

How I rate this week out of 5

1   2   3   4   5

"Stress is caused by being 'here' but wanting to be 'there'."

Eckhart Tolle

Week Commencing / /

Top priority this week:

My 3 daily habits to track

1. ....

2. ....

3. ....

Tracker

M	T	W	T	F	S	S
M	T	W	T	F	S	S
M	T	W	T	F	S	S

To do

_____
_____
_____
_____
_____
_____
_____
_____

Notes

MONDAY

TUESDAY

WEDNESDAY

THURSDAY

FRIDAY

SATURDAY

SUNDAY

How I rate this week out of 5

1   2   3   4   5

"Every day brings a choice. To practice stress or to practice peace."

Joan Borysenko

Week Commencing   /   /

Top priority this week:

My 3 daily habits to track

1. ....

2. ....

3. ....

Tracker

M	T	W	T	F	S	S

M	T	W	T	F	S	S

M	T	W	T	F	S	S

MONDAY

TUESDAY

WEDNESDAY

THURSDAY

FRIDAY

SATURDAY

SUNDAY

To do

- _____
- _____
- _____
- _____
- _____
- _____
- _____
- _____

Notes

How I rate this week out of 5

1   2   3   4   5

"Every day brings a choice. To practice stress or to practice peace."

Joan Borysenko

Week Commencing   /   /

Top priority this week:

My 3 daily habits to track

1. ....

2. ....

3. ....

Tracker

M	T	W	T	F	S	S
M	T	W	T	F	S	S
M	T	W	T	F	S	S

To do

_____

_____

_____

_____

_____

_____

_____

_____

Notes

MONDAY

TUESDAY

WEDNESDAY

THURSDAY

FRIDAY

SATURDAY

SUNDAY

How I rate this week out of 5

1   2   3   4   5

"Life is really simple, but we insist on making it complicated."

Confucious

Look where you are in life, where you have been and where you are heading. Take time to reflect on what you have accomplished — small or big — which makes you proud. What is next for you? How can you make things even better? Remember to celebrate even the small wins!

Monthly Planner

M	T	W	T	F	S	S

Goals and priorities this month

My Notes

Date:

_____

_____

_____

_____

_____

_____

_____

_____

_____

_____

_____

_____

_____

_____

_____

_____

_____

_____

_____

_____

Week Commencing   /   /

Top priority this week:

My 3 daily habits to track

1. ....

2. ....

3. ....

Tracker

M	T	W	T	F	S	S

M	T	W	T	F	S	S

M	T	W	T	F	S	S

To do

- _____
- _____
- _____
- _____
- _____
- _____
- _____
- _____

Notes

MONDAY

TUESDAY

WEDNESDAY

THURSDAY

FRIDAY

SATURDAY

SUNDAY

How I rate this week out of 5

1   2   3   4   5

"Nothing is impossible. The word itself 'says I'm Possible'."

Audrey Hepburn

Week Commencing   /   /

Top priority this week:

My 3 daily habits to track

1. ....

2. ....

3. ....

Tracker

M	T	W	T	F	S	S
M	T	W	T	F	S	S
M	T	W	T	F	S	S

MONDAY	
TUESDAY	
WEDNESDAY	
THURSDAY	
FRIDAY	
SATURDAY	
SUNDAY	

To do

_____

_____

_____

_____

_____

_____

_____

_____

Notes

How I rate this week out of 5

1   2   3   4   5

"A journey of a thousand miles begins with a single step."

Lao Tzu

Week Commencing   /   /

Top priority this week:

My 3 daily habits to track

1. ....

2. ....

3. ....

Tracker

M	T	W	T	F	S	S

M	T	W	T	F	S	S

M	T	W	T	F	S	S

To do

- _____
- _____
- _____
- _____
- _____
- _____
- _____
- _____

Notes

MONDAY	
TUESDAY	
WEDNESDAY	
THURSDAY	
FRIDAY	
SATURDAY	
SUNDAY	

How I rate this week out of 5

1   2   3   4   5

"You cannot change your destination overnight, but you can change your direction overnight."

Jim Rohn

Week Commencing   /   /

Top priority this week:

My 3 daily habits to track

1. ....

2. ....

3. ....

Tracker

M	T	W	T	F	S	S
M	T	W	T	F	S	S
M	T	W	T	F	S	S

To do

_____

_____

_____

_____

_____

_____

_____

_____

Notes

MONDAY	
TUESDAY	
WEDNESDAY	
THURSDAY	
FRIDAY	
SATURDAY	
SUNDAY	

How I rate this week out of 5

1   2   3   4   5

"For what it's worth, it's never too late to be whoever you want to be. I hope you live a life you're proud of, and if you find that you're not, I hope you have the strength to start over."

F. Scott Fitzgerald

2024 Calendar

	Mon	Tue	Wed	Thu	Fri	Sat	Sun	Wk
	25	26	27	28	29	30	31	52
January	1	2	3	4	5	6	7	1
	8	9	10	11	12	13	14	2
	15	16	17	18	19	20	21	3
	22	23	24	25	26	27	28	4
	29	30	31	1	2	3	4	5
February	5	6	7	8	9	10	11	6
	12	13	14	15	16	17	18	7
	19	20	21	22	23	24	25	8
	26	27	28	29	1	2	3	9
March	4	5	6	7	8	9	10	10
	11	12	13	14	15	16	17	11
	18	19	20	21	22	23	24	12
	25	26	27	28	29	30	31	13
April	1	2	3	4	5	6	7	14
	8	9	10	11	12	13	14	15
	15	16	17	18	19	20	21	16
	22	23	24	25	26	27	28	17
	29	30	1	2	3	4	5	18
May	6	7	8	9	10	11	12	19
	13	14	15	16	17	18	19	20
	20	21	22	23	24	25	26	21
	27	28	29	30	31	1	2	22
June	3	4	5	6	7	8	9	23
	10	11	12	13	14	15	16	24
	17	18	19	20	21	22	23	25
	24	25	26	27	28	29	30	26

	Mon	Tue	Wed	Thu	Fri	Sat	Sun	Wk
July	1	2	3	4	5	6	7	27
	8	9	10	11	12	13	14	28
	15	16	17	18	19	20	21	29
	22	23	24	25	26	27	28	30
	29	30	31	1	2	3	4	31
August	5	6	7	8	9	10	11	32
	12	13	14	15	16	17	18	33
	19	20	21	22	23	24	25	34
	26	27	28	29	30	31	1	35
September	2	3	4	5	6	7	8	36
	9	10	11	12	13	14	15	37
	16	17	18	19	20	21	22	38
	23	24	25	26	27	28	29	39
	30	1	2	3	4	5	6	40
October	7	8	9	10	11	12	13	41
	14	15	16	17	18	19	20	42
	21	22	23	24	25	26	27	43
	28	29	30	31	1	2	3	44
November	4	5	6	7	8	9	10	45
	11	12	13	14	15	16	17	46
	18	19	20	21	22	23	24	47
	25	26	27	28	29	30	1	48
December	2	3	4	5	6	7	8	49
	9	10	11	12	13	14	15	50
	16	17	18	19	20	21	22	51
	23	24	25	26	27	28	29	52
	30	31	1	2	3	4	5	1

First edition published December 2021
Version 2.0
ISBN: 9798779661607 (paperback)

www.sensorywellbeingot.com

Printed in Great Britain
by Amazon

23064763R00090